IMPOSSIBLE THINGS

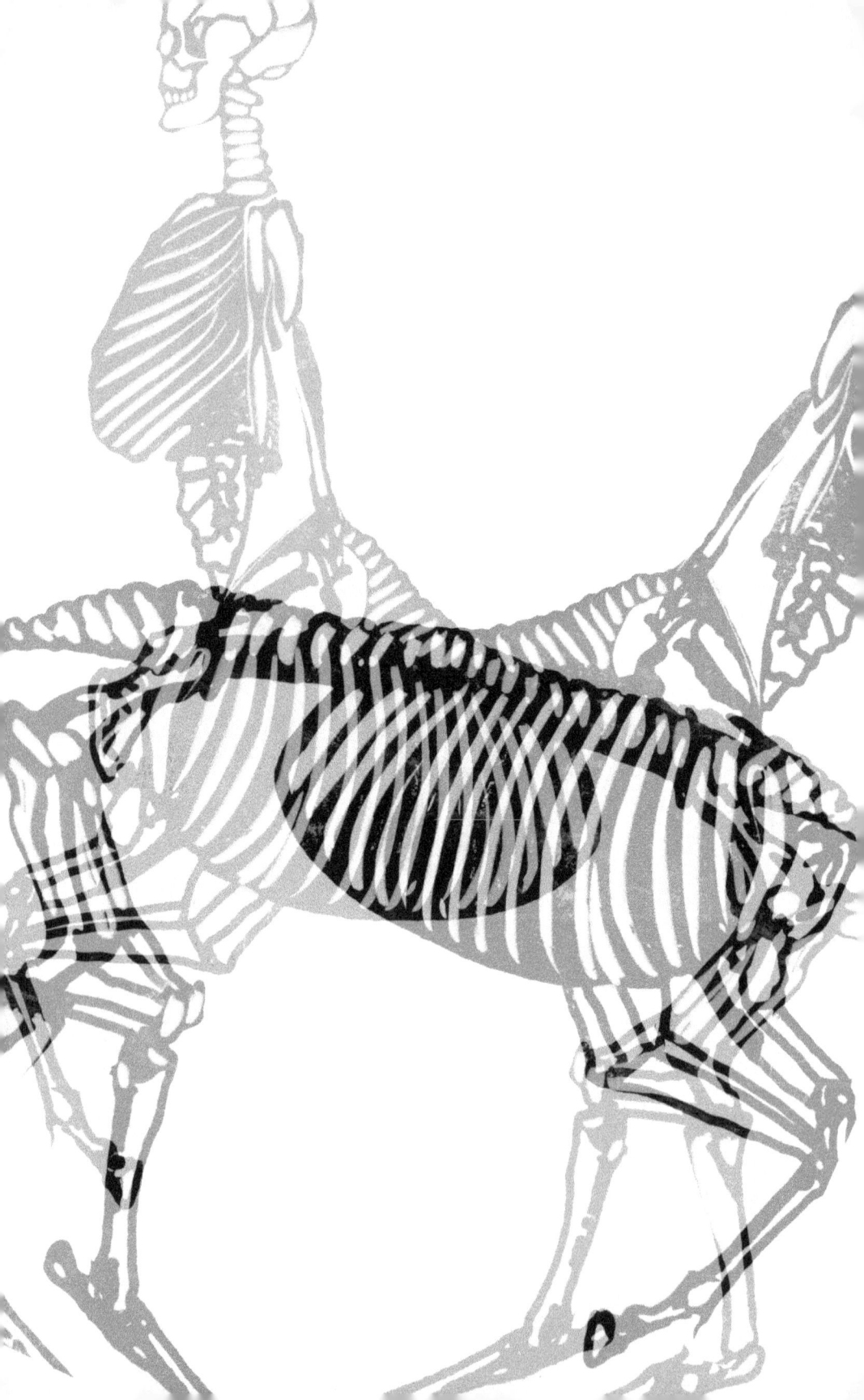

IMPOSSIBLE THINGS

MILLER OBERMAN

Duke University Press

Durham and London 2024

Project Editor: Bird Williams
Designed by Dave Rainey
Typeset in Untitled Serif and Trade Gothic LT Std
by Copperline Book Services

Library of Congress Cataloging-in-Publication Data
Names: Oberman, Miller, author.
Title: Impossible things / Miller Oberman.
Description: Durham : Duke University Press, 2024. |
Includes bibliographical references.
Identifiers: LCCN 2024005707 (print)
LCCN 2024005708 (ebook)
ISBN 9781478031093 (paperback)
ISBN 9781478026860 (hardcover)
ISBN 9781478060086 (ebook)
Subjects: BISAC: SOCIAL SCIENCE / LGBTQ Studies /
Transgender Studies | SOCIAL SCIENCE / Death & Dying |
LCGFT: Poetry.
Classification: LCC PS3615.B476 I476 2024 (print)
LCC PS3615.B476
(ebook) | DDC 811/.6—dc23/eng/20240626
LC record available at https://lccn.loc.gov/2024005707
LC ebook record available at https://lccn.loc.gov/2024005708

Cover art by Sheyam Ghieth

Only when our memories have turned to blood within us, to glance and gesture, nameless and no longer to be distinguished from ourselves—only then can it happen that in a most rare hour the first word of poem arises.

—RILKE, from *Journal of My Other Self*

I've always felt sorry for those with only one limited way of viewing their past.

—VAGINAL DAVIS, from "Creative Time Summit DC," 2016

In memory of

Mark Robert Oberman ז״ל and Joshua Oberman ז״ל

May their memories be for a blessing.

CONTENTS

xiii   Dedications

xv   Prologue: Two Lunches with my Father

1   All These Beloved Books

2   *Memoir I*

3   Joshua Was Gone

6   *Memoir II*

7   The Wind Is Loud

8   *Memoir III*

9   *Memoir IIIi*

10   *Memoir IIIii*

11   The Pool, 2019

13   *Memoir IV*

14   Proper Identification

16   Joy

17   "if this was a different kind of story id tell you about the sea"

19   *Memoir V*

20   Taharah

21   *Memoir VI*

22   Twenty-three Facts about Joshua's Death

23   *Memoir VII*

24   Dear Mr. Pennypacker

25   Commas

26   Joshua's Birthday

28   *Pottstown Mercury*, 1972

30   *Memoir VIII*

31   *Memoir IX*

32   *Memoir IXi*

33   History of Fingers

36   Odo

38   Theory

41   Phoenixville, 2020

43   The Centaur

44   Giant Bird

46   *Memoir X*

47   On Similes

48   Comes With

50   Two Photographs

51   *Memoir XI*

52   *Memoir XII*

53   *Memoir XIIi*

54   The Field

62   You Are a Field of Little

63   *Memoir XIII*

64   *Memoir XIV*

65   This and That at the Frick

66   How to Sleep

67   *Memoir XV*

69   *Memoir XVi*

70   Catskills Poem

71   The Camels

72   *Memoir XVI*

73   Two Shabbats with Paul Celan

75   *Memoir XVII*

76   Northport

78   Syntax, 2022

79   Joanne Dies, 2017

80   *Memoir XVIII*

81   Jewish Cento, 1957

84   Epilogue: Mensch

87   *Memoir Cento*

90   *Memoir Cento i*

92   *Memoir Cento ii*

94   The Cake

97   Notes

101   Acknowledgments

DEDICATIONS

This book borrows from an unfinished one by my father, which has no dedication page. He may not have known how to grapple with the impossibility of a dedication, given the subject matter of his book. He may simply not have gotten there yet. I tend to think of the last sentence of his book as a kind of dedication. "May you all find peace on your journey," he wrote.

To all of Joshua's siblings, Jennifer, Jesse, Eli, and Jaime, and the beautiful families and communities you've made. I know you each carry your own wildly different kaleidoscopic memories of our family. I'm endlessly grateful to you for your patience while I've explored my memories, and always want to hear yours.

In memory of Jan Oberman ז״ל, thank you for sharing your stories with me.

To Seth Anderson-Oberman, a most rare and beautiful man and father.

To Susan Oberman, who always comes with.

To Eli Oberman, I melteth to pure wode without you.

To my beautiful children, Rosie and Reuben, who guide me with joy and hope, and who keep me *very* humble.

To my partner, my *bashert*, Louisa Rachel Solomon, my greatest source of love and courage.

To all of you who have lost children, siblings, and parents.

To the brave queer and trans writers who came before me, and those who write alongside me in time. My body and my words are truly impossible without yours. Thank you for lighting the way.

A final dedication: this book, which I turned in to my editor on October 1, 2023, grapples with the way that trauma caused by the death of a single child ripples through a family for generations. Now, witnessing an ongoing genocide in Palestine and being confronted with the reality of thousands upon thousands of dead children, the lens through which I view my own book has irrevocably shifted. Some of these poems took me twenty years to write, as I sifted through complex feelings of trauma and grief. Time, what a luxury. Time to mourn, bury our dead, sit shiva. Time to care and be cared for by our loved ones; this is time everyone should have, and yet today Palestinians often lack access, not just to food and water, but even to the bodies of their dead. I'm overwhelmed with awe as I watch Palestinian poets and journalists writing and responding in real time to mass and individual death. These writers are true heroes. I dedicate these poems to all writers of conscience and witness and to all those who see the loss of every single human being as the loss of an entire world. The unthinkable, preventable loss of these children and families will be felt and mourned for generations. May we all find the strength to keep witnessing, may our hearts be strong enough to keep breaking. May each of us do all we are able and more, in the streets and on the page, to bring about an end to this genocide and a free Palestine.

PROLOGUE

TWO LUNCHES WITH MY FATHER

On March 31, 2006, my father died at age fifty-nine, of lung cancer. He spent the final year of his life working on a manuscript called *Climbing the Joshua Tree: Awakening the Heart to Move through Sorrow* about the mysterious death of his first child, Joshua, at age two, and his journey to grapple with this loss through mindfulness meditation.

Before he died, he asked me to read it. I got through less than a chapter. I had little interest in his spiritual journey and found his Sufism appropriative at best. He had recently taken me downtown for pizza and, dragging his oxygen, which he couldn't get around without by then, tried to open up to me about the book and Joshua. I recall him saying, "When Joshua died, my heart closed," and that's when I stopped listening. Fuck you, your "heart closed," I thought. What about me? What about my childhood? The material felt doubly hurtful—in how it was *and* wasn't true. The truth that he had been shut down during my own childhood was painful, and I wasn't ready to think about it as an adult. The fact of his fixation on this as the Truth, when it was only partially true, seemed to pave over the reality, for me, that this hadn't wholly been the case. In some ways, he had been a wonderful, open-hearted father. His statement felt cruel, and I resented his need to say something about himself without thinking of how it might sound to me. Trying to read the book confirmed this erasure: there was hardly a mention of me, my mother, or my living siblings to be found, except in ways that had to do with his continued grief around Joshua's loss. This was about *his* journey, *his* healing. But to what end? Not, it seemed at the time, to become a more loving father to his living children, of which there were four.

As I sit here today, in January 2018, my own firstborn child, Rosie, is two years and one month old. She is on nap strike this week, whooping gleefully in her crib. In the fall of 2005, I stood with my father in the pantry by the grill tools, by the door to the back deck he'd built. A between-places place. Not in the house, not out on the deck. It's falling off the house now, the deck. A hazard. It was new then. He asked me if there was anything I wanted to ask him about before he died. *You might want to know something later*, he said, *but I'll be gone. How can I know what*

I'll want to know in the future?, I said. I had a few thoughts, but they all sounded too petty in my head.

I was twenty-five. I was thinking of another day he'd taken me to lunch, at a Greek sandwich shop called Café Europa. I'd come home from my first year at college and was trying to talk to him about my gender, the ways I'd been bullied. I described men chucking bottles at me from cars, and a woman who, cross-ashed on her forehead, spit in my face at a Metro North station that spring, calling me a *faggot*. He looked worried and gave me terrible advice. *If you only add a few more feminine aspects to what you wear*, he said, *it will help. You don't even have to wear a dress! Just a pair of dangling earrings would probably do it!* I knew he loved me. I knew he didn't have any idea how to love me. I stopped trying to talk about my gender.

There's nothing, I said, in the pantry. *I can't know what the questions will be. I don't have them yet.*

As I sit here again, on another today, my second child, Reuben, is two years and three months old.

After Rosie was born, I began to experience anxiety. I'm sure all new parents do. Mine began to approach a kind of anguish. I called my mother and asked her if she had a copy of my father's memoir. I wanted to ask him about Joshua.

This book includes excerpts from my father's manuscript, which I've distilled and lineated, setting pieces of his descriptions of the days surrounding Joshua's death among my own poems. As a young adult I often felt guilty I didn't call him more. Now I'd give anything to be able to call him. This book is a kind of call, an attempt at a shared story. This is about fatherhood, although when my father died, he did not know I would become either a man or a father. Today, November 7, 2021, Joshua would be fifty-one. My father would be seventy-five. Hi, Papa, it's me. It's been a long time. Putting all these dates down is unlike me, but you do it often in your book. Trying to mark time, I suppose, trying to find something concrete to hold on to, a habit it seems you began in the hours and days following Joshua's death. Time: what a terrible choice for a reality check. If you were here, I'd tell you everything I've learned about time since you've been gone, how lyric it is, how elastic, how queer.

It has taken me a long time to write this. It keeps on not being what I want it to be. Today is February 20, 2022. At first I wanted to figure out the mystery, what happened to Joshua, my father, my siblings, me. I began with an investigation, chasing down houses, local newspaper articles, police reports, the names at the scene. Patrolman, doctor, neighbor. I didn't get far. People died, records were lost, phone calls unanswered. I kept logs in my notebooks, what I sent, who I called. Little came back. Joshua's obituary and official death report are all I have. I look at the pages of notes and remember the sound of a dial tone. How it wavered and bent if you listened long enough, the sound of a phone off the hook, flatlined forever. This is a story about how we get stuck in time, or parts of us. Pain nails us to a spot, and when we move from the spot, the nailed-down piece rips off. A piece of my father at the pool where he found Joshua's body. A shred of me nailed to a plastic chair in a sandwich shop. The state of Pennsylvania has yet to unearth a police report for me; they can't even agree on what county Joshua died in. So I set to work collecting these other pieces, stuck as I am in the pantry, a nonroom my mother allowed to be cluttered. It was for storage, after all. An extra freezer, boxes of folding chairs. To the right of the screen door, a wardrobe that still had its skeleton key.

On July 16, 2005, Joshua's birthday, my father began his book with this sentence: "My first-born child, Joshua, was born in 1970 and died when he was 2 years and 2 months old. Today, he would be 35 years old, older than I was that day in 1972, older than some parts of me today, which remain nailed to that moment so long ago" (1).

Fitting, this image, since my father worked as a framing carpenter in those days. He also loved poetry.

He began his book with a Rainer Maria Rilke quote:

Perhaps everything terrible is in its deepest being
something helpless
that wants help from us.
—Rainer Maria Rilke, *Letters to a Young Poet*

All These Beloved Books

gently strewn around me are about death.
Paul Celan is writing about death and
Cheryl Boyce-Taylor is writing about death.
Pamela Sneed is writing about death and
Kiese Laymon is writing about death.
Wendy Xu is writing about death and
I want to read the book that tells me how
to wedge a candle in a slot of air just so
to make a gap for my father to come through
tonight, just this once. I have so much to
ask you, Papa, so much to tell. I have
cooked you a fat steak and you don't
have to worry, being dead, about your
cholesterol. This is a heart-healthy meal,
O decomposed one. You are nothing
but chambers of unblocked light. Talk
to me. You've got acorns all over you,
Virginia creeper grown up through the soil
above what was once your hands.

Memoir I

I am twenty-six
                    Joshua

                        going everywhere

            groceries   lumber

blackberries   fields

            working   Joyfully

red tomato   green ones

I am in love

I am in love

with being important to him[1]

Joshua Was Gone

And in his place   one royal blue Ked
        on the floor of Papa's closet
under the hanging   button-down shirts and sport coats,
        houndstooth and herringbone.
In among his softball cleats   his favorite slippers
        his green-stained mowing-the-lawn
sneakers   his mahogany tasseled loafers
        a tin of boot wax.
I sat there rarely   and always alone
                to touch it.
There in the lacquered dark   in the smell like leather
        soaked up the sun
then leaked it out gradually   I looked at
        my dead brother's shoe
the zigzag tread   pretty worn
        the dirty white rubber trim and shoelaces.

And in his place   we played fiery lava
        we played stick knife fights
capture the flag   hide-and-seek.
        We played kittens
in the laundry basket we served tea
        in tiny painted cups
Papa carved and painted   pick-up sticks
        and we carefully picked them up.
We fried marbles   saw them sear and crack
        we hunted amethyst quartz
I retrieved a baby   bunny snared in the pricker bush
        and we fed her with a syringe.
We played jacks   jinx, Wiffle ball, rummy
        wink murder, and we sang.

And only one picture of him   in the long hall of many
          that looked even longer then
in the top left   corner of one collage.
          He looked golden
brown eyed and gleaming   bronze little fox.
          He looked out awarely.
He looked like a toddler.   Face of a puzzle
          face of a pip
face of an orchid   mouth of a plum
          jaw of a hill of waving wheat
chin of a quince   neck of a gentle mountain
          collarbone of wind over water.

And in your place   an empty place.
          You, can I call you you?
Gone boy   never to outgrow a sneaker
          a faded picture.
And if Papa wept   lit a candle some calendar day
          you were born or died
I didn't know about it   Papa's pain kept private from me
          zipped up and boxed
quelled, jarred   let out in jags maybe
          or concealed
in ordinary rages   stubbed toe
          or someone left a fan running.

Never was he here   and never my brother.
          Except in the hall
in the closet   in an old ghost story of impossible things:
          locked windows
door swollen in its jamb   his terror of water
          the fact
he had never   climbed over his crib rails
          and nevertheless that night climbed
past his mother who was not mine
          past his father, who became mine

4

all the impossibility   arranged in its narrative skin
        going always to memorized nowhere
as if the story itself   always told the same
        or typed on his old Compaq
always the list   of impossible facts
        years later, might keep Papa
from finding him   that September morning
        given its impossibility
in the neighbor's pool.   If no month September
        if no night
no grass   no water
        if no state Pennsylvania
if wood didn't release   instantly its vapor
        and the door swing free?

I never inquired   how they loved him,
        He no one to me
just the gone kid   never truly gone
        Such long time went since
time moving   through the house
        the night wet-green underfoot
dew on his sleeping clothes   his feet.
        Time the hole
time shivering in red-brown edges   who ripple then push in
        drowning in the night
the lock outside my door   hook-in-eye screwed tight
        when I turned two
so in the morning when I woke   I must cry out my upness
        such little lungs fizzing in oxygen.

Memoir II

Joshua isn't   in his crib

I am awake   I run

"Joshua! Joshua!"

The front door   The dogs

> *Frantically*

> *Searching   scanning*

the landscape   our bodies melting

> *endless search*

I am far down our country road

> *Calling   calling*

> *"Joshua! Joshua!"*

Then   screaming   home

arrow   true flying toward

the target

The Wind Is Loud

The wind is loud on the water today
I think about him drowning

I walk to the store for a bottle
of wine I think about him drowning

I read to Rosie before nap
in the rocker where he's drowning

I make her a peanut butter sandwich
cut in triangles think about him drowning

I rinse her little blue plate and spoon
in cool water where he's drowning

I get up to pee in the night
with the light off and he's drowning

An old woman throws crusts to gulls
in their descent I see him drowning

Wondering if there's a word for how birds
all move together drowning

Thinking about my father thinking about him
drowning I think about him drowning

Memoir III

I reach our neighbor's home

                        their son is holding Joanne

he grasps her there

                in the middle of the road

she is struggling

                  pointing to the unfenced

ground-level pool   in the back

                There is Joshua

lying on his back beside the pool

                    like pale blue marble

Perfect   beautiful   lifeless

        like a copy of Joshua

            I touch him

            I lift him up

cradle   and rock

Memoir IIIi

I reach

      in

               in the back

        Joshua

lying   *beside the pool*

Perfect

       I touch him

       I lift him

Memoir IIIii

   reach

         in

                  in

             Joshua

lying

Perfect

The Pool, 2019

No not that one, this other one—they'd
loved it, the Mirantes, the family who lived here before
us, this aboveground beast of rusted struts and blue
plastic sheeting, on a bed of sand and brick. For $100

and beer my nephew drained water into the alley,
sawzalled posts and stacked bricks in a corner, got
a text from his friends, who came over and helped
with the bricks and the beer, and got more texts and left,

the pool's blue ruins still heaped on the sand. Winter came.
We attended interior things. Unpacked our boxes, painted
rooms jonquil and lavender, seaworthy and pearl.
We hung skillets, scraped frosted vinyl from windows,

found dust and dusted it and made more, changed
diapers and did laundry. My nephew, who would also have been
Joshua's nephew, and would have called him uncle, stayed awhile
in the basement, and Joshua, if he were here and an uncle,

turned fifty, and in the corporeal world and unbeknownst to me,
ants took up house in the pool's ruins. I found whole worlds
there come spring, the blue skin layered into an unplanned
and wild town in the sandpit, gritty with grease and chemical

buildup, from bottles the Mirantes saved for us in the garage:
Golden Glop, Imperial Black, and Blue Seal, not knowing we'd
never move in until the pool came down, looked at it sideways
as if it might move, looked back at our baby still in arms,

our cheerful toddler bounding around the daisy bush. And now
these blue sheets of ants swirling shocked at being lifted
and exposed to the sun, to me, my trash bags and scissors, my eyes.
Victims of genealogy as many ants must be, caught up in a story

of a boy who drowned through no fault of theirs, or mine.
No fault of anyone still alive. I cut the pool to rags, long
filthy strips, and bagged it. It took longer than I thought.
It was heavy work, and dirty. And there was my father watching,

not a next-to-me ghost, not in the yard, but in my cutting
hands, in my mouth spitting sand, in my eyes blinking grit
as I ended that pool. Here we are, Papa, trembling
in our tendons, shredding it shredding it shredding it.

Memoir IV

An ambulance

Men   like planks of old lumber   warped

air thickdark

The men keep their heads slightly bowed   necks rigid

only moving their eyes   they cross the yard

past the pool that swallowed Joshua

the men turn   carry Joshua away

it is so still you can hear the grass break under their feet

Although I don't know it
this is the last time I will see Joshua

Proper Identification

All branches of Judaism discourage the viewing
of the body other than for proper identification.
We are encouraged to remember our beloved ones
in the vibrancy of their lives.
— *The Jewish Mourner's Handbook, 1992*

The last time I saw my father   not in a dream   he was
    shoeless   he was in his box and shroud
I stood there remembering   someone
      I think my brother   told me   when you see
a dead body   it's clear the person is gone   that some
    ineffable thing   the soul maybe
is gone   I stood
    and waited   to feel the certain absence of his soul

I lost track of time   I thought maybe it had been too long
    and I should go back   to help my mother with
something   or maybe someone else needed a turn
    with him how   had I usually   before that now been
tracking time   it was a big room   I had walked through
    a door and   then a short dark tunnel   like in the theater

his body at the front   a stage behind   someone had draped
    fabric over a big crucifix   but I could see it underneath
the room had a high ceiling   I looked up and then down
    at his body many times   the ceiling was too high
and not high enough   every time I looked up then down
    his body was still there   how long now?

would someone come to tell me   I took too long?
    he looked like himself   he felt like a magnet

14

or a hole I was falling into   I both wanted to and did not
      want to touch him   I would not get another chance
I wondered was I scared like "chicken" to touch him
      I did not have the feeling   my brother or whoever

said it to me said   I'd have   It wasn't clear to me at all
            It was him there   him and all that meant
him who yelled   him who made me   so many sandwiches
always such big bursting ones
      embarrassing sandwiches   to take to school
if he wasn't in his body   why could I not walk away
            from it   my bones   fuzzy and hollow

what had been clear to others   was not clear to me
            Was I stalling?   I couldn't tell
if I wanted to leave   and couldn't
      or thought I should   and didn't want to
how to tell was broken   I thought about playing
      long-toss   at the old Crozet School ball field
each taking a few steps back

after each throw   getting farther and farther apart
      "bless my good right arm"   Stanley Kunitz said
in "The Testing-Tree"   he never knew his father
            I looked up at the ceiling and took a few steps back
I stepped back and back   it was spring
      the air crystallized with pollen   the grass so tender

so crushable   so low   you're almost afraid
      to walk in it   but only now
then you couldn't be afraid   that way   because
      you were too young   for that kind of fear
and because   your father had thrown a ball
            and you were chasing it

Joy

Like the time I dreamt about a loon family
just some common loons—not metaphors
in any way, just real loons in a lake swimming
near each other so it was clear they were a set,
preferring each other's company in the cold
still lake with its depth of reflected pines.
The curve of their black heads and sleek
necks, black-and-white stripes then checks
on their folded wings, floating so low
atop their reflections they almost seem
inside them. Their wails like wolves, their
calls like an echo without origin, their
calls like an echo of lake, or what makes lake
lake. How nice to think the male and female
loons cannot be told apart by their plumage
and that they build a nest and sit on eggs
together. One of their calls is called *tremolo*.

"if this was a different kind of story id tell you about the sea"

—Marwa Helal, after her poem of the same title

1.

I look at it every day and still can't tell you much. Today a figure out on the jetty is shadowboxing, hitting wind, running down the boulders that break it, crouching in crevices, springing up to kick spray. It's beautiful, but not only. I'm too tired for similes this morning. What, I want to ask, did air ever do but hold you, what did waves ever do but be tireless, come and come, come and come?

2.

I learned this as a child. Dirt and sand, air and waves treated me the same as everyone, my body not expected to be like anything, free from meaning aside from being. "What are you?" the green broad leaves asked no one ever. The sky boundless blue or domed gray and spitting ice hit every kid the same, those whose skins and names and genders lay neat as feathers, vanes perfectly directed outward from the inner quill, and those of us whose plumes seemed disarranged.

3.

I dislike to speak of it, I may dislike speaking of it more even than I dislike it to have happened that on this island where I was born those boys quietly climbed [   ] behind my back and [   ] my swing at its apex. The air held us all the same though I was not the same, that was their point when [   ] I not seeing gone flung [   ] in air, layers of gases, water vapor I was not [   ] harder than any other in the elastic scattering of light and gravity while [   ] watched and turned away in [   ] let us practice punishing and being punished. I have thought since then how sensible that the word *shame* begins with the same sound that ends the word *punish*. That mute shuffle, the edgeless shadow, the convulsing shake of a diaphragm with all its wind knocked out.

4.

I want my children, your children, even those boys' children uncrushingly to fit within their structures, but how good a father can I be when last summer at the beach I saw two boys chucking a football, shirtless and seeming joygold and free as the waves and I felt pangs at their perceived ease, knowing nothing of their troubles or fears. If only my blood beat even as the sea, faithfully lapping in valves, foaming safe in chambers. Now I am a man, I remind myself. And those are not the boys, any of the boys who had me choking on the lightness of air. My father had ease like that, at least in photos. After he died I tried to write a poem that imagined all my selves as separate bodies, each standing on the shoulders of the previous one. It was mainly a description of shoes. A good place to try this would be in salt water, but I don't see time that way anymore, at least I don't want to. I want something less ponderous, less vertical, like how the sea cannot fall down, and I would forget their names and stand in the surf like a gull.

Memoir V

Joanne and I   ask each other   questions:

How do you explain this   Joshua had never   climbed out of his

crib   Why hadn't he stopped in our room   How had he wound

up at Ed and Martha's unfenced pool?

                                  Why would he go in the water?

He hated water—baths, wading pools, any water

Ed and Martha overslept—if they had been up   getting

ready for church as usual   they might have

heard   Joshua

Taharah

I'm wondering about you, *chevra kadisha*,
the "holy society," who will prepare my body,
once I'm no longer in it, for the earth.

Will you know me already, or see me for the first time
as you wash and shroud me, as my father was washed
and dressed in simple white *tachrichim*, for those

about to stand before God—Perhaps by then I'll know
if I believe in God. I like the democratic
nature of the shroud, an equalizing garment. You

may see a body that surprises you. You may not have seen
a man's body like this one before you, which I hope is very old,
wrinkled, and (since I'm wishing) fit, muscled

as much as an old man can be. You'll see scars.
Ragged dog-bit forearm, elbow my father picked gravel
from over the sink, then flushed with foaming iodine,

and the long double horizons on my chest, which trunked my body
like a tree. If I am unexpected, let me not seem
grotesque to you, as I have to many people, perhaps

even my own parents, and others whose highest
kindness was to say nothing. Please let me return to dust
in peace, as the others did, and recite those beautiful psalms,

remembering, as you go about your holy ritual,
how frightening it is to be naked before another,
at the mercy of a stranger's eyes, without even any breath.

Memoir VI

Joshua is buried in a simple pine box. We aren't invited to see him alone before the funeral service. The casket is closed, which, we are told, is customary for children who have died. I miss my father, who still hasn't been contacted.

Twenty-three Facts about Joshua's Death

1. Joshua died in Phoenixville, PA
2. after wandering
3. from a farmhouse
4. in a U bend of the Schuylkill
5. on Dreibelbis Rd
6. in my father's youth
7. 138 feet above sea level
8. according to Patrolman Ronald Pennypacker
9. Arthur Nicol glanced out his window
10. and saw the body in the pool
11. He was pronounced dead at the scene at 8:30 a.m.
12. by Dr. DeWitt Dabback
13. who himself died in 2015
14. whose father emigrated from Turkey
15. who fought in the Battle of the Bulge
16. who never learned to swim, though once thought he could, in a salt-water pool
17. to his surprise he sank like a stone in a freshwater pool
18. Dabback delivered one thousand babies
19. and people say he didn't charge them if they couldn't pay
20. He checked Joshua for signs of life
21. there were none
22. Regarding weather, the *Pottstown Mercury* reports that "the dense cover of dampness obscured the sun throughout the day, except for a few brief moments in the afternoon when the sun cast a feeble shadow."
23. Regarding Kepner and Romich Furniture, whose ad appears beneath Joshua's obituary: "Kepner and Romich Furniture sells every year enough wall-to-wall carpeting to cover Route 422 from Douglassville to Limerick!"

Memoir VII

    a young man

                in need of comforting

                I don't want to be seen that way

Suddenly   *my mother making   animal sounds*

        grunting   growling   *hissing*

higher-pitched wails   the air at the top of the stairs

deep red

Her   *wail breaks*

        distorted   collapses

My mother in the bathroom screaming at God

My mother must be on fire

        filling up the   room   body twisted

        spread out asymmetrically   hands clenched

crazy hatred filling her

My open right hand   through the flames strikes her

She gets smaller

I turn my back on her and walk out

    It is only time

Dear Mr. Pennypacker

Please forgive this intrusion from a stranger

I am wondering if you are the same

Mr. Pennypacker from September 18, 1972.

> I am watching, from Louisa's grandfather's favorite chair,
>
> rain slanting down over the Catskills.
>
> It looks like rain in a painting, long gray lines.

Did you by any chance work as a patrolman in Phoenixville

taking, poolside, the neighbor's statement on finding

my brother Joshua's body in the water?

> The rain has stopped and the little white butterflies
>
> are flitting around the clouds of hydrangeas
>
> that one tree sticking up from the mountain like a cowlick.

I am writing a book about my father, that's all, and

there are so few left alive who remember that day.

People keep dying and do not return.

> Have you noticed the state road there in Phoenixville
>
> is dead-ended now by the river, chain-gated,
>
> the house unreachable as a sound?

Commas

Came home and I found my typewriter
case a little crushed it's my fault
probably for leaving it looking like
a stepping stone for someone not tall
enough to climb onto the toy chest
but who very much likes to clamber
up there my father built the toy chest
for me and now the result is my comma
key sticks won't fly up to make its mark
so no more clauses of that tender
kind or just imagine them there or figure
out how to use a semicolon or type the word
comma when I need one lots of things
are called commas not just punctuation
a certain butterfly a bacillus responsible for cholera
the chest's nails are slowly withdrawing I notice
pulling themselves out in the invisible
hammerclaw of time or else the wood itself's
ejecting them feeling maybe hey it's been long
enough let me just be planks again or it could
be the climbing itself did I also climb
and all that climbing's worked
against those nails a little each time after
my father held one in his hand one in his
mouth and with his hammer made a box

Joshua's Birthday

Was on Shabbat this year, and I made fried green tomatoes.
Rosie helped me pick the four biggest, careful not to knock

yellow flowers, or smaller tomatoes. Reuben, nearly two, helped
by not throwing them, and eating cereal quietly as we cooked.

Rosie mixed the sauce: buttermilk, pepper, chives, salt, garlic.
I set up the flour dredge, bowl of beaten milk and eggs,

then cornmeal and herbs, and into our biggest skillet,
flashing with oil. We cover the challah, pour juice and wine,

clean out candlesticks. Now begins the two-month corridor
between Joshua's second birthday and drowning. This time next year

I'll have forgotten the exact feeling of living with a two-year-old.
The sudden anguished screams over what an adult would call

nothing. The way Reuben bounds everywhere, calling
hello to neighbors sweeping stoops, meowing at cats, yelling

thank you to the workers picking up trash, bouncing around
calling *shockum bockum!* in excitement, randomly lunging

at my legs to hug them. His passion for pushing furniture
through the house pretending to mow grass. The totally erratic

zeal as he tries dragon fruit or just a glass of water and declares
I LOVE IT. Want Papa, he says, at bedtime these days, as he kisses

every person at the dinner table, then clings to my neck.
Joshua had just learned not to pick green tomatoes, that summer,

but they are delicious, acidic and firm, rich in the dip Rosie was so
proud to have made. It won't be the same, remembering, as being

in it, I think, as we sing, light candles, and try to kiss
our children's heads, one of whom still allows it, saying

be who you are, and may you be blessed
in all that you are and all that you will be. Amen.[2]

Pottstown Mercury, 1972

Vol. 41, No. 301 September 19, 1972

Reports the wait for Cease-Fire in
North Vietnam, and that "President
Nixon Hikes Oil Quota," and late
baseball scores: Dodgers and Padres
scoreless after 1 inning. The weather
report: "considerable cloudiness today,
fair tonight and Wednesday chance of
rain 30 per cent," and Joshua's name
under the heading "deaths."

"A 2-year-old Phoenixville area
boy drowned Sunday morning
when he wandered from his
home and fell into a neighbor's
swimming pool.

Joshua Oberman, son of Mark
and Joanne Oberman,
Dreibelbis Road, Phoenixville
RD 1, was pronounced dead at
the scene by Dr. DeWitt Dab-
back, 17 N. 4th Ave., Royer-
sford, at 8:30 a.m.

Upper Providence Township
Police said the child wandered
away from his house and
crossed the road to the property
of Arthur Nicol.

Nicol glanced out his window and saw the body in the pool according to Patrolman Ronald Pennypacker. He rushed out and pulled the child out of the water, frantically attempting to revive the boy as others called for help."[3]

Memoir VIII

For a week we stay at home and receive visitors Joanne's

pregnancy complicates   grieving   people use it

*   to evade   reality   Joshua is dead*

Her pregnancy   leverage to block   falling

into

Memoir IX

How   haunting   frames my circle   How

had Joshua climbed out of his crib? How had he slipped past our

room? How had he opened the front door? How did he get to the

pool? How had he fallen in: had one of the dogs pushed him in by

mistake? And   the repeating   dismay that

he who hated water   drowned

Memoir IXi

How   *How*

had   *How had he slipped*

  How had he opened   *How did he get to*

  How had he

And   *repeating*

  water

History of Fingers

My *zayde* lost some toes   in a mower as a boy   years
      earlier than when he took   the name Jay   when he
was still his parents' Isidore   child cantor   who sang in shul
      pried wax out the candlesticks Later he met my
grandmother   Eleanor   Later my Papa was born   then
      his brother Jan   who years beyond
being born   lost one   construction   and then my Papa
    lost   all Joshua's   and then I had Rosie   and took her
      to an ordinary   place with chairs walls
where she held a hunk of lavender quartz

Let's pause there   go back to Jay's toes   they never bothered me
      gone so long   Let's veer   equivocate   People tell
untruths about scars   could do that here   The pock on Papa's cheek
      from a venture west when he was eight
(the story goes)   they stopped for lunch
      on the red desert sand   he and Jan explored
fell down a hole   were chased by monkeys   who shot
      arrows at them   as from Oz   They ran My father bravely
shoved Jan out of the hole   was shot   face marked but my father

lied about his face   After he died I asked his brother   who said
      it was Jay's story   lifted   characters shifted
It was Jay fled the flying primates armed with bows
    Jay with the scar   empty toes   I reel back   squat low
hover   drift   So much desert could be   was
    The upper Mojave 1955   Egg salad   pickles   rye
Brothers who fought   backseat-cramped-hot   restless as their mother
    yelled   Overhead the Vaux's swift   who like to swirl and
mass at dusk Roadside   Joshua trees   cholla cactus hedgehog
    cactus   spiky ocotillos leopard lizards   legless lizards
side-blotched lizards   zebra-tailed lizards
      Greasewood   The yellow creosote flower

which smells of rain and tar and smoke at once   some of its bushes
        almost twelve hundred years old   Shall I name all the snakes?
Rosy boa   Mojave shovel-nose   in the creosote scrub   I know
        so many words but none   for the sound my child made
when the hydraulic   medical table lowered on her hand   which she'd
        just placed on it   momently   to steady
her walk   back to her chair   around the exam table
        Only just turned   three after all   That chair unreturned to
she'd hoisted   herself up on   expertly before
        then   full of wonder   came to see how a table could
hold a body   move up and down   I was there for my back
        she was there because I was   that's how it is
It was a scream and more than a scream   scream of the realization
        of unfixability itself Unended tunnel dropped down
no place to land   no monkeys Just a hole
        Hole with a scream in it   Hole with a hand in it
        hole with   a father in it   hole hole

Gap   burrow pit   ruptur fissur schism
        Did I jump in   yes I jump in
I go fast and do things   In   down   shouting
        button-pushing   raising a trap off
prying crushing parts up   Iron   carbon   zinc
        My arms many   and strong   as a squid
Fishing softly   it out of the scissor lift   Holding that body in my own
        holding that small hand still   holding parts and holding
parts of parts   Soft tiny pisiform
        proximal phalanx   distal phalanx   scaphoid

        bless the little lost ones
        bless the EMT who put a hand on my back
bless gauze and tape bless wheels   bless the little
        bones I saw   bless wailing lights   blue white blue
white bless thread   bless needle   bless the blades that cut
        the little hoodie off   the dog one   deep blue
with matching sweatpants   bless pants   bless blood inside

34

and out   bless that woman   made the ambulance fly
bless my own bones   muscles   hands who didn't give out
        bless axles   bless shock   bless the pizza we almost ate
bless snakes   bless

            forgetting
        Mojave green   northern desert night   diamond-backed rattler
great gopher   They are here doing   that belly-flexing huffle
        curve   to call me down   the hole again   each rib
wave-bending   coiling   locomoting   unlimbed
        Tell me about lunch I said   in the ambulance   What did
mama make you?   What did Zo have?
    When we went   to the aquarium   which did you love
better otter or eel?   It might not have been   the Mojave
        where they had lunch   I made that up   It could've been
any barren wind-place   as they moved from the Bronx to California
        for one year only   Or they never ate   in the open air
it was a highway diner   gleaming a great chrome beacon
    off the exit ramp   And if they never moved   back to PA?
known for the aquatic   hellbender   the hemlock   the brook trout
    where would I be? My father and mother then   never met
and me not here   in this ambulance   not here at all

Odo

I've been thinking of Odo again,
            the changeling on *Star Trek: Deep Space Nine*, the shape-
                  shifter who can be—or appear to be—anything:
                       Tarkalean hawk, trip wire, plasma, chair covering,

but who must, every eighteen hours, rest in his original gelatinous state.
            Once this happens in a broken turbolift in the folds
                  of Lwaxana Troi's dress. It hurts him to hold
                       human form too long. He does not want to change

in front of her. This is private. He does it, usually,
         in a bucket. The bucket looks like a slightly
                futuristic trash can, narrower at the top than bottom,
                     golden and glossy. I thought of this, obviously,

because I want to be liquid in a pail. Solitary.
        Slosh once and be dissolved, regenerate.
                But I'm unsettled by the scene in the elevator.
                 Troi is kind, softly asking questions. Odo

turns his face away, sweating and leaking apart. "I did not
      grow up," Odo tells her, of his early years being
               studied in a lab, "it was merely a transition
                  from what I used to be, to what I learned to become."

He describes trying to fit in, changing to entertain
      scientists at parties: "Odo, be a chair. I'm a chair.
          Odo, be a razorcat. I'm a razorcat," he says, letting out
             involuntary moans of pain.

She ask what she might do to make it easier.
      "Nothing," he says, but then she removes
          (though it is no equivalence) her wig, and somehow,
             this helps. "Let go," she says,

"I'll take care of you." And he looks up,
      at what I don't know, takes a gulp of air,
            and becomes a shimmering gel, briefly still
               human-shaped but metallic,

translucent, boneless, glowing red where
      a human heart would be. And pours
            into her dress, which she has gathered up
               for him to rest in.

Theory

> Gender is, thus, a construction that regularly conceals its genesis;
> the tacit collective agreement to perform, produce, and sustain
> discrete and polar genders as cultural fictions is obscured by the
> credibility of those productions—and the
> punishments that attend not agreeing to believe in them.
> —Judith Butler, *Gender Trouble*

Yes they chased me   Yes it was spring   It was spring
        It was spring   It was   spring all day and night
All the trees leaning   into light their fuzzy buds and calyxes
        The grass greener than whatever's greenest
The daffodils yellow and yellow and yellow and cream

This telling will be different   I swear   from when I was eighteen
        and described the perfect   springiness of the grass
under my high-tops   Fuck the lyric   mountains and the air
        I had just turned ten   We were playing capture the flag
when the boys in my class   and their older brothers   turned

In the mock Olympic Games   I'd won javelin   shot put
        and wrestling   Came second in long jump   but that
didn't matter now   they chased me   I fled past the echoing
        concrete of the pavilion   past barrel trash cans fizzing with flies
fizzing with flies   past the short field   over the edge of Ragged Mountain

That's the real name of it   I say the real names of things
        when I know them   Maybe somebody said a name then
Maybe to Ethan   lithe as a deer Ethan my friend who'd given me
        a folding knife for my birthday   smiling quietly
or otherwise their blood   moved them like magnets   like swallows

or certain bugs that hang together like nets   fly like they're
        woven together   Maybe someone said *dyke* or *goy*
their names for me   A boy who had just started shaving gave a whistle
        gestured with his arm   My body pressed against
the mountain's steepness   They are so high above me

I can see the soles of their shoes   when they lift them up to kick
        dirt and leaves in my face   zigzag   swoosh honeycomb
head of a fanged roaring wildcat   They stone me   stone stone stone
stonestone   When I wrote of this before   I focused on the rocks
        gave their scientific names   suggested I was becoming one

Naming things feels good   cataloging has great colonial power
        and so distracting   A way of looking away
They threw and threw   All the roly-polys   from under the rocks
        revealed and   scurrying
No one came   No one stopped them   They stopped maybe

because they got bored   At first they got farther away as they threw
        Someone   heel-dragged a line in the grass and they stood
behind it   Humans in a field   Men in the man-made ground
        keeping at bay below the tree line's dark   dangling
edge something else   Something not made like them

or unmade   abject and profane   I heard a sound from my body
        like a growl   heat poured off my head   I felt my
personness evaporating   as the boys laughed upright
        in the mown field   I bellied up with millipedes   snails
last year's leaves rotting and skeletal

The body lost human speech then   But somewhere someone
          was writing   I know that now   at a desk in a cool room
shining haired   You can't see them now   you in the bloody torn
          jeans   covered with mountain-stuff but you will   They are
explaining it   That these boys   Ethan   Noah   Shawn

big blonde Jeff who once   picked you up and
          stuffed your whole body in a trash barrel
in a week's worth of discarded lunches   maggots   broken
          glass and who claimed   to have seen a movie
called *Carnal Knowledge*   but wouldn't describe it

They are explaining it all   in a book   They are saying
          you are a person   who came first
not a copy   They are saying   these boys   are fictions
          stoning other fictions   These are *the punishments*
that attend   These are ghosts throwing at nothing

Phoenixville, 2020

1.

I want to see the house where it happened, but the address I have
seems too simple, from another time. Dreibelbis Rd, Phoenixville,
Rd 1. From my Queens garage, I look for an old farmhouse in a U
bend of the Schuylkill River. I travel the lockdown, pandemic way,

following the road on a screen until it dead-ends. The photos taken
in full summer, lush fields, trees leafed out. I drag my mouse until
Upland Way forks right and Dreibelbis with no explanation
is gated and chained: "Road Closed. Authorized Vehicles

Only. Strictly Enforced." Stuck in the overgrowth, branches
sagging into electric lines, I zoom in until leaves pixelate, my eyes
fuzzy as seed dandelions. I try to go around, search street, aerial.
Past Old State Rd, left on 113, left again on Dreibelbis in the bent

elbow of the river. I try satellite, topography, and elevation maps.
Feet above sea level: 138. Barometric pressure: 101 kPa. What
did I think I'd find here? My father? My brother? A nursery,
windows closed, no curtains whipping in the no wind over no crib?

2.

Originally called Manavon, Phoenixville was later named after
Phoenix Iron Works, itself originally called the French Creek
Nail Works, the first nail factory in the US, renamed in 1813 after
the owner saw an image of a phoenix in the factory's blast furnace.

Right there in the Nail Works flames, a phoenix. A mythical
bird that looked like an eagle, but with feathers of gold and red
which lived for half a thousand years before burning entirely
to ashes on a funeral pyre lit by the sun and stirred by its own

wings, only to emerge from its ashes, begin another life cycle.
In another version of this myth the phoenix consumed itself to ash
on the altar at the temple of Helios in Egypt and a worm
emerged from the ashes and became the baby phoenix, reborn.

You would have loved that, Papa—the bird that becomes the worm
of itself. I imagine you riffing puns off the Rivingtons 1963 hit,
"The Bird's the Word," maybe "the bird's the worm"? In Dryden's
translation of Ovid's *Metamorphosis*, the phoenix has no parents,

is born only of fire, of and from itself. Flame-made, consuming,
consumed. I look for you in Dante and Ovid. I translate five hundred lines
of the Old English poem "The Phoenix" looking for your house.
"Lifelong" "it feeds" "only on drops of incense and amomum"

Dante says. "He burn'd, Another, and the same" Ovid says.
"Its final winding sheets are nard and myrrh" Dante says.
"Casia, Cynamon, and Stems of Nard . . . He liv'd on Odours"
(Ovid) "That vapor, vigorous, shall crack the mist" (Dante).

"From his tender Wings shakes off his parent dust" Ovid says.
"The dust of him collected by itself" Dante says.
"Of Bodies chang'd to various Forms I sing," Ovid says.
"It is asserted by great sages," Dante says.[4]

The Centaur

First they called me *it*, and then, ignorant of how my people
use this word, they mashed up the meager nouns
they had for gender and called me *the goy*, and said
to not be one or the other was to be nothing.
It ate the grass it was shoved in, knelt at salt licks.
It took the barbs and kicks and crushed them into
fur and leather. Oiled and burnished, it made those
halves into one galloping body. Horse and rider.
The centaur endured the school-day, cruel gray rag, filth
stiffened. The boys and girls who fit so easily in their costumes
looked like stick figures, crude and two-dimensional.

Dante already knew, it read later. In *The Inferno*, in the seventh
circle of hell, centaurs guard the river Phlegethon, one of Hade's
five rivers. Phlegethon: river of fire, river of boiling blood,
which boils forever the souls of those who commit violence
against their neighbors. Centaurs guard the edges, shooting
arrows at any of these sinners who try to move to the shallows.

When sometimes I wish I'd had a boyhood, I remember those
days instead, my four muscled legs. I was seven feet tall then,
riding myself, carrying myself. A centaur is never lonely.[5]

Giant Bird

I have a friend who used to say
she wished a giant bird would come down,

rarely and irregularly, to take someone away.
She is a person I consider truly kind,

puts glasses over house spiders to gently
nudge them onto paper and take them outside.

She thought fear of the giant bird might help us,
that knowing it might come take us, or our

neighbors or loved ones, would make us kinder,
more joyful. But wouldn't cancer do that? I said,

or someone hit by a bus? A brain aneurysm? No,
she said, with the bird, it would be different.

And sometimes I saw her looking up at clouds,
or out over deep, deep water, eying horizons,

perhaps thinking of it, the giant bird that will
come, flapping and shrieking, to remove

one of us villagers. I don't think of it much
anymore, except every now and then if I am dog

tired of my own suffering, like last week, when,
shirtless on the exam table, getting an EKG

to find out if I was having a heart or panic attack,
the nurse, seeing my chest scars, asked, in shock

if I "used to be a *girl*?" and then asked if my parents
"were OK with me," and told me about the one

other trans person she'd met, a woman, who "even"
"was pretty" and "even" "had a normal boyfriend,"

who was "even" "good-looking." I thought it might be
a great time for the giant bird to come take someone away.

Memoir X

I wake up and get dressed, but my clothes feel like they don't fit me right. My shoes pinch my toes as I walk downstairs. My arms swing and my shirt talks back to me at the shoulder and under the arms. Everything feels too tight.

On Similes

I have read my father's book and, as I suspected, much of it is bad.
Especially the attempts to teach mindfulness, which,

given that once at a bakery he listened at length to a woman
from a mindfulness class he taught gush about its effectiveness

all the while standing on my mother's foot, is no surprise to me.
Especially bad are the similes.

"Grief is like an unkempt beggar" (242).
". . . sniff these last days of summer like a fine wine" (242).

This compared to when he's not trying so hard.
When, at forty-two, he has a heart attack and his father comes,

"he holds me as if I'm made of smoke" (109).

Comes With

Like many people I have a mother.
She has always been and remains
a big gasper. The gasps are loud
and not a little scary. They sound
extreme. Like if you found out something
so shocking or one last breath before
your ship went down. The other day
in torrential rain I very slowly backed
her car into a fire hydrant someone had
against good sense painted white. It was
surprising. She gasped, like if you learned
of a coup in your country or if waiting
for the subway someone shoved you close
to the platform's edge where you stood
holding your baby. Sometimes I feel anxious.
My brother says it's not the truly frightening things
that cause the gasps. "Where do they come
from?" I ask him, "Is it hereditary?" But
neither of us recall our grandparents doing it.
"Maybe," I suggest, "she gasps for the whole family,
all its known and unknown shock, for all
assimilated German Jews who trained
themselves to golf at country clubs, decorate
trees indoors at Christmas, and never
under any circumstances to gasp. Maybe
she does it historically, for them all."
My brother finds this generous. "It's
about control," he says, "or lack thereof,
and a transference of the helplessness
to affect the truly terrible things
onto the mundane." And that ended
the matter, though not of course the sound.
And who would I be without it? Calmer,
less jumpy, or nothing at all—as if that gasp
were the lines in a poem that never seem

right, but without them the poem loses
all meaning. Now, or even earlier is where
I'd usually describe the sound. I view lyric
description as an important part of the poet's job.
I tried "rocks against a rasp," or "frozen wind on a file
sucked through a chipper-shredder," or "inhaling
broken glass." Perhaps I'm too close to the sound.
Like how growing up, currant jelly chicken "comes with"
string beans almondine. Everything had something
that "comes with" and only now I realize it wasn't
limited to dinner. The gasp and life are linked.
Sound lives in the body, currents
through cells, gales in the throat.

Two Photographs

I find a photo on my mother's table of my father and Joshua
at the beach. I've never seen it before, it's the only
photo I've ever seen of them together. They're in the surf,
my father looking impossibly young. Joshua looks about
one. He's naked, our father holding him above a wave,
another rolling in.

                  My father's family frequented the Jersey
shore—in a photo of his grandparents at the beach
they stand in the middle distance looking as unlike beach-
goers as is humanly possible. All in black: shawls, suits, boots,
hats. Walking wardrobes ruffling in the wind. What a distance
from that photograph to this one.

                      How did my father learn
to be this beautiful? He is shirtless and smiling, and they
say Joshua hated water, but he looks happy here. *You
can be here forever*, I tell the snapshot. The photo quality
is bad, grainy, as if a mist or veil is obstructing
its clarity, or this moment of simple happiness is too much
to ask of the light-sensitive chemicals that make this magic.
Their faces escape me. I want to go in, share this moment
as two fathers, two sons, but it's too blurry to enter. Not for
Joshua, though, he is there forever, safe in arms.

Memoir XI

her family sends all of Joshua's furniture to the Salvation

Army   All his toys and clothes   his

room   repainted   New curtains   New furniture

I don't resist   I hardly notice

I look up the next week   there is hardly a trace

of Joshua left behind

Memoir XII

And where is Joshua?   Each day I am flooded

he puckered his mouth   a certain way when

he was concentrating   his cute two-year-old-walk

his   obsession with a red plastic motorcycle   he rode

all over   "vroom vrooooom!"

Memoir XIIi

Joshua   *I am flooded*

all over

The Field

> Often I am permitted to return to a meadow
> as if it were a given property of the mind
> that certain bounds hold against chaos
> —Robert Duncan, "The Opening of the Field"

1. Windows

Through the window, in the nearly empty room
another building, window, nearly empty room,
bald and institutional, a long tube of cold
fluorescent light—not a thing to call a bulb.
Bulb: a certain shape—an onion,
a subterranean bud, a root. The air is clean
enough today, though my head is dull as a sandbag.
Cramped chest, empty room.
I am responsible for a human life.
The breadth of it is crushing. Grand open space
outflung endlessly in time, the way, each morning,
I fling out the quilt over our bed, how it hangs in the air
as it waves three times, maybe four, to sort out
the wrinkles and disarrangement of the night,
until it settles over the sheet with some evenness,
like a field.

Mornings, oatmeals, naps, afternoons at the aquarium
where walls turn to lit water, fish flash iridescent, rays skim
graceful as hawks, or outside by the sea, sand
blowing low against the child's uncovered face. Nights working
or cooking or talking or watching the game while she sleeps,
knowing how little my life would be worth, should anything
happen to her.

And then, close behind that thought, or preceding it,
of Joshua, finished at two. The late understanding
that all I knew of my father was this afterlife,
whose shadow country hangs like rubble in the corner
of my vision field, salt-sown.

Empty room, empty field, hold bounds.

2. Tomatoes

Where do I go to know my father? To the house
of his first wife, not my mother, in rural Pennsylvania
where he worked at the turkey farm, where Joshua wandered
into the night and drowned? To his grave in the woods, or to
Joshua's grave, now next to his mother, who had him exhumed
and moved, then joined him? Or to the field behind the first
house I remember, the one he cultivated with orderly
stakes, string trellis of sugar snap peas, little hills
of squash and flowers?

Or to the field beyond that field, dead gold grass
boneyard of gone milk cows
picked clean by crows, bones marrowless, light and leached
in the untended scrub.

My guts untended as that field.
Past the mulberry tree dropping purples
in the greasy parking lot, past the back-alley mechanic,
Pitbull chained at the shop's mouth: the dead field my father
left me. All he planted and tended in every yard we shared.
Joshua had just learned, that summer, to pick a red tomato,
leave a green one. He often sang in the garden, my father.

3. Computer, 1988

I used to try to play "Hitchhiker's Guide to the Galaxy"
on the Tandy 1000 in my father's office, for which he had
the second disk only, not the first. I'd sit in his desk chair,
slide in the big floppy disk, light and flexible as green birch
and watch the shock of power in the screen as it booted.

The game was all text. It went like this:

Field   Score: 0   Moves: 0

You are in a field.
>walk

You are in a field.
>walk right

You are in a field.
>walk left

You are in a field.
>walk left

You come to a cellar door in the ground.
>open cellar door

Cellar is pitch black.
>go down

The cellar is pitch black. You hit your head.
>go right

You walk into a wall.
>leave cellar

You are in a field.

4. The Fire

My father burned the field behind our house
and almost burned the mountain too.
It started as a country burn pile; leaves and brush,
blown-down branches from winter storms.
He'd laid down clear arcs of gas
glugged out from the push mower's
red can as I watched from afar, banished
as too little, chucking the rain-sogged
rubber ball against the mudroom bricks,
waiting for the blaze. The frightening glory
of smoke and flame burst like Virginia
poppies escaped their neat rows in the median.
Roused and running the fire ate the field. Green
then flame, then white, then black and moving
up toward the tree line, where our yard
ended and became Tom Mountain.
I stopped throwing the ball and was still.
As if the fire owned movement. My father
looked far away, jerky, the fire much bigger
than him, stomping at rills of flame. Then
deer leapt the leaning orchard fence. No,
not deer, men. With buckets and hoses,
men who tended the apple trees, sure-footed.
They stretched the hose over the fence,
they filled and passed buckets, filled,
passed, doused, and it was done. My father
drove to Crossroads Store to thank them
in beer but they didn't return and that beer
sat so long in our pantry we moved, and winter
turned the burned field brown, and the ground
frosted and froze, and the daffodils came
back, and we moved again, and I became
a man, and my father died, and terrible
fires burned in California and those men
never came back to be thanked but not
necessarily in that order.

5. Field Cento

All summer you mowed the grass in meadow and hayfield
   the mowing machine
deep in the day, in the deep of the field
a series of caesuras/a fractured field.
I will constitute the field
that is a field folded.

It is summer, the rhetoric of the field
were fields, a river, and beyond, more fields,
wood of his forests and stone out of his fields,
the field moan
of misty fields, by their sweet questionings.

Deep until this snowfield's pocked
white on the green fields, the startled cows
seeing throughout the field no man not touched.

The field is not
a new cosmic skeletal reprieve, afloat amongst the forces
   of the primeval lightning field.

Vigil strange I kept on the field one night
made in possession of the field,
this field, and tended it awhile
over the breathing field
It could have been a field
I grow weird in the field,
the opening of the field,
my field, O my field.

There is a field. I'll meet you there.
My father carries me across a field,
leave this thrashed field, and be smooth.[6]

6. Definitions

Field, meaning "open country," in Old Frisian *feld*,

      in Old English *feald*, a fold, an enclosure,

in Old Dutch *felt*, in Middle Dutch *velt*.

      Land unencumbered by obstruction

of trees or marsh   or hill or building.

      Flower of the field   beast of the field.

A place, first, for uncultivated plants, then cultivated ones.

      Airfield battlefield   butterfield   snowfield

wheatfield field of coal bleaching field   firefield

      turnip field   questionfield, question-filled, question-

feeled. Something open and enclosed at once, cultivated, or un.

In chess, the playing area, and later, the part of the board

      to which any given piece may move, and later again,

the king's field. Field of vision, depth of field, which until recently

      I misheard as "depth of feel," which I took to mean,

obviously, how tactile the depth of a photo seemed, how far in

      it seemed touchable.

Field as surface, expanse.   Field of stars, field of sea,

    ice field. An open place, for planting, or resting, and where

you can, given vigilance, see what's coming at you.

You Are a Field of Little

You are a field of little
flowers in a field of
      little flowers
      stems and petals

You are a bed of little
rivers in a bed of
      little rivers
      I mean mirrors

I mean stems and petals
feathering liquidly
      clean as imaginary nature
      but rushing in real water

River free from drowned cans
in a little field of flowers
      where we see first the lights
      then the bang that made them

Memoir XIII

I return to work in a week. My boss, Roy Varner, a kind man, has given me a week off with pay although I am a relatively new employee. It feels good to return to my work as a framing carpenter.

The men I work with are awkward around me, unsure of what to say or how to behave. They split off into their own circle and joke and kid around as they always do, but quiet down when I approach.

Bobby has two kids and talks about them all the time, but I don't hear any stories now.

I feel ashamed, as if Joshua's death is a sign I wear on my chest, which says in bold letters: FAILURE.

Memoir XIV

For moments, I forget   I feel part of something

ordinary   easy   more alive in my body

    the paces of hard work framing out houses: carrying

lumber nailing together partitions   kneeling to strike a

chalk line   guiding a wheelbarrow filled with cement

using a level to   frame out a door

This and That at the Frick

I bring my students to the Frick to see Frank
O'Hara's beloved *Polish Rider* and after giggling
at the work Bronzino did on the silver-painted crotch
of *Lodovico Capponi*, whose silk sprouts like a big
snail or scrolled bedpost between his legs, we walk
to the West Gallery and all agree Rembrandt did a grand job.
The young man is handsome, his horse handsomer, especially
its head. The rider looks like he could dismount, meet O'Hara
and Ashbery at the San Remo or Cedar for drinks.
I get it. But across the hall, El Greco's *Vincenzo Anastagi*
despite every frippery draws no titters.
Graying at the temples, he is armored at the chest and arms,
with a white ruffle around his neck. It escapes
his sleeves, too, bloomy as the rind of stinky cheese,
or egg whites whipped to stiff peaks.
Against this froth his uncultivated face, midlength
beard, dark eyes, maybe kind, maybe sad. The green
velvet of impossibly puffy shorts does nothing
to lighten the weight of his eyes, nor does cloth
billowing behind him, a drapery from nowhere
come to hold him in relief. A color I can't name. Not
red, not purple or brown. Like blood in a dream,
oiled as bone broth. What a strange word,
relief, which used to denote the body
of a dead person or any kind of remains, but now
means ease, deliverance from pain, or the impression,
in art, that a thing is raised above a surface. Vincenzo
is all these things at once, and I can't wait to bring Louisa
here—Louisa, who this morning on the train said *gross*,
reading over my shoulder O'Hara's description of
"laborers" who "feed their dirty / glistening torsos."
Gross, she said, on the B train going over the bridge,
meaning O'Hara's reduction of these toilers to objectified
working-class trunks, and she was right, they're never
just beautiful, these old things, these men's things.

How to Sleep

I the air and stars and you the moon,
Rosie, dirty-fingered in the pages.
The ocean at night, the open
window, curtains, waves.
Seagulls and pigeons dark in the dark.
We two in the white rocking chair
under the framed Catskills tourism cat,
mountain-pawed, green and purple-eared
peaks, soft and wild over the mirror lake
and phone number for information:
1-800-882-C.A.T.S. Outside: wind,
time and tomatoes still green globed
among their greener scented leaves
on the balcony next to boxes of basil,
next to mint, our fingers still herbal
from the afternoon, water in the red can.
Your night lamp, blue and ship shaped,
now without light, and I a song, and Mama
a prayer, and all of our hands on our eyes,
your bed cool and the sheet smooth
from my hands over it, sheet of sails,
clouds, water. Nothing undone.
Salty wind around song-light,
scent of green tomatoes and the sea,
the Catskills above us, red sun
setting in the painted lake.

Memoir XV

In three months   Jennifer is born   healthy

The dread of something going wrong

                  like an enemy with a pistol cocked

Had the grief and shock   done   harm

          We are unable to relax around the baby

keep   to a constant watchfulness   awake and

                      asleep

The sight of water   pools   the ocean even

        baths makes me

tremble

Joanne's tension is greater   Her need to guard

burdensome and excessive to me

I feel she is always watching me that she doesn't trust me

with Jennifer for one minute

             omnipresent gnawing

something I could have done

I constantly relive   that September morning

I'm still running down the road   I'm

holding Joshua in my arms   looking into those lifeless

dull blue eyes that had been so sparkly and alive

Memoir XVi

Jennifer is born   healthy

                            awake and

                     asleep

water   the ocean even

               baths

tremble

I feel

with Jennifer

                  omnipresent

I'm   running down the road   I'm

   holding Joshua in my arms

      so   sparkly and alive

Catskills Poem

Outside, there's nothing going on. It's so good. Crickets
cricketing. The last of the hibiscus flowers, huge as hats,
their leaves turned to lacework by nibbling aphids,
grasshoppers, caterpillars. Light on the late-summer
mountain and various greens. Your grandmother,

who lived so long, has gone on before us, but her potted
palm remains here, on a little slatted wood stand with wheels.
Someone hammering something up the mountain. Strike,
afterstrike. I close my eyes and breathe, and when I open
them again, the world gets greener and greener.

Some parts of the air are cooler than others. The mountains
breathing all over me, some breaths warm from sunned
leaves, others cave-cooled, exhaled granite. The hawk
up there feels it too, tilting over the mountain, so
casual, regular as breathing to fly like that.

I hope, if you're reading this, you aren't waiting for me
to say something profound. A poet once told me
it's enough to just describe the world. Is it? I'm trying
too hard again to make a poem into a door. *The door*,
I used to say when I was a child, *is a JAR!*

The Camels

Louisa had already run into the ocean.
Rosie and I were walking down slower
when a woman pulls up in a truck
with two camels. Single humped, almost
too bright to look at, each tuft of fur
a magnesium flare that should hurt human eyes,
but doesn't. One camel rises on two legs,
picks Rosie up and holds her. Rosie and the camel
look at each other. "He never does this,"
the woman says, as the camel puts Rosie gently
down. Everyone goes for a swim and later
I run down and up the mountain's steep back,
hauling wood for our fire. The woods
fragrant and cool: sharpraw pine, vetiver.
My legs without any pain. Without memory
of pain. Everyone doing their own thing, and that
thing good enough, and without memory
of the feeling of not-that. Louisa singing
shoulder to shoulder with one camel. Both
camels sitting by the fire, incandescing.
They were humming, like they do.
They were not real camels. I know that.
They were too small, delicate, eyebrows not
bushy enough. They might have been llamas.

Memoir XVI

The world   the same as always   yet my place in it

different   rules of gravity   changed

it's hard to raise each foot off the ground then it's

reversed and I'm   floating   hardly in my body

I think I see him being led through the mall by other

parents and rush after them

I'm here so he must be here

I sit dully in the afternoon sun rehearsing the word dead

Many months pass before

Two Shabbats with Paul Celan

> arrowy one, when you whir toward me,
> I know from where,
>
> I forget from where
> —Paul Celan, "A Ring, for Bowdrawing"

One Friday it sunned all over
the catmint and coneflowers,
then I read Celan and grew concerned.
"The stone behind the eye,"
he wrote, "it recognizes you,"
"on a Sabbath." At first
I thought *you* was him but
what if *you* was me?

This is from "Vinegrowers," his
last poem, worked April 1–13,
1970, in Paris. He has gone and left
the work to others, drank from
his last earthcup and leaned
into the river to be drunk instead.

Paul Celan took to the river,
returned to the elements.
I always wanted to be an element,
indisputable as stone, inarguable
as wind and water. Are you thirsty?
Are you seen by that eye-stone?

Every morning I get dressed
in memories of words that told
what every part meant: a girl's arm,
breath, a girl's mouth and chest.
Nothing escapes: not electrical outlets,
razors, shirts, ships, gingko trees,
god.

Snow furls down the mountain,
past the prison, river, vineyard, grocery.
Horizon-dividing. The stubble field
cut to a quarter of itself. As soon as
I can't see it I forget it. In the light wind
snow falls, unquestionably, up.[7]

Memoir XVII

I had loved our big old stone house

        one of Joanne's friends   heard

several small children from another time

     singing nursery rhymes

in the hallways   in our new baby's room

One   night   windows closed   Jennifer's room

began to whistle   curtains flutter and flap

covers   pulled from Jennifer

by an invisible force   she is being dragged

from her crib   We flee   We are afraid

     afraid

Surely they   know we   have gone mad

Northport

I dreamed I was in the house on Elwood Road, which was not,
in the dream, knocked down, and had an attic full of furniture, things

left behind by those who died. My Aunt Mary's soft flowering
bedspread and one of her famous leaf T-shirts, made by carefully

collecting what dropped off sugar maples, scarlet oaks, beeches,
the needles of the resinous pitch pine, dipped in paint and pressed

into fabric, making ordinary shirts, three to a pack, a day in the woods.
There was a big wooden principal's desk, wardrobes, chifforobes.

I recognized a child's chair, small, plaited cane, and behind it
the rocking horse my father carved for me, mane suggested by S-

shaped curls of wood, nose pointing delicately to the wardrobe
in which hung one of his shirts, looking, as he'd no doubt

describe it, were he here, "like new." One of his favorites:
the long, pointed collars of the 1970s, Irish wool, plaid

green and blue, verdant. It makes me smell moss, little streams
running through the forest, just to look at it. My father's brother

keeps one of their father's sweaters in a zippered bag, opening it,
rarely, to breathe his father, closing it quickly so the scent isn't

used up. I look down at my feet to see if they are there. They are,
and below them, the rest of the house. The bedroom I shared

with my brother, testing the strength of my legs by pushing
my feet against the upper bunk and lifting it up and down.

The bathroom where my mother soaked my feet in hospital tubs
of warm water and Epsom salts the summer they cramped

from growing pains. The layout of the house can't be right,
it's huge and mazelike, as if someone kept adding on rooms.

The den I drifted down to one night after I'd been put to bed,
to crouch outside the doorframe as my parents watched

Moby Dick in the dark. Gregory Peck's terrifying intensity
as Ahab, looking inhumanly tall as the ship rolled over billowing

waves, an angry sea. Dozens of sailors throwing roped harpoons,
grim and desperate as the music swelled. I took a deep breath,

right into my feet, and went back upstairs. Attic, shirts,
window with a little blue square of sky, bloom of rain clouds

in the distance. It was all happening forever, spinning.
Someone shows you how a container of yogurt has fruit

on the bottom you can mix up, and the world is shot
through with cherries. I reach out to touch the shirt—

Syntax, 2022

The woman whose land my father is buried on
has died.
The woman on whose land my father is buried
has died.
The land belonging to the woman my father was buried on
has died.
The land my father is buried on, the woman it belongs to
has died.
Belong*ed* to. Died is the land my father is buried,
died is
the woman whose land.
Died is
my father,
died is
the scrub woods in winter. The woman whose woods we buried him in
has died.
She was a nurse, a teacher. She was very tall, a painter. I never really
knew her before she had died.
Those who knew her lit lanterns and buried her on the hill, the burial
hill
for those who have died.
I do not know if it's the same hill we buried my father on when he
stopped
breathing and died.
I know less and less. My father would have laughed to hear me saying
that if
he were here not died.
Sometimes it's confusing to remember who is aboveground, who
has died.
What is the grammar for this? The pines, upright trees or cut planks
who died
making their boxes. It is good to have simple trees, tools, words when
they died.
Lanterns to light, many lit wicks on a hill until the flicker of live flame
has died.

Joanne Dies, 2017

I never met her. My father's first wife, mother
of my siblings Jennifer and Jesse.
They ask us to join them at her funeral, and we do.

And there in the pouring rain in the spring
at the grave, as I step aside to let those
who loved her shovel mud, I see it: she had

Joshua's grave moved. "Joshua," the stone reads,
"beloved son and brother." My brother, I think,
standing there holding my baby in the rain.

Memoir XVIII

my left hand down on all things sacred and holy

the right one to the Courtroom of Nature and swore to

protect my children and family

Yet my very existence now   testimony   fact

I had failed to uphold the basic directive: KEEP THE BOY ALIVE.

No matter how badly I raised him, no matter how inept my

parenting   he   as long as he lived   transcending

my mistakes   his own destiny   He could

follow his   gifts   to their rightful

conclusion

> *What age qualified as the end/death place that meets the criteria certifying that I have done my job: forty? fifty? seventy-five? Certainly not 2.*

Jewish Cento, 1957

1.

There is a hill and on that hill is a stone.
     My ancestors step from my American bones,

from the day of our fathers' fathers.
      I have become a lost name
as anonymous as grass.
      Bread for the breathers' need,
cast thy bread upon the waters, says Ecclesiastes.

And it was evening, and it was morning,
      and let him come singing,
and like thy father sing in tunefulness.

Tender and tuneful is the short name,
     your songs are carried heavenward, I gather
the world is full of cherries,
     and the rugged places shall be made level.

O men, be like a rosebush,
      rise like a great bird, like a lifted promise.
Over and over, when the wayside dust had grayed us,
     our Father, our King, remember we are dust,
the rushing and undulant sons of fire.

2.

You are not here.

        You can speak on equal terms with God,
and in the dark of absence your full length,
        your lion's head grows old, your hair—
the winds are blowing through your lofty places.

He left behind him. A hole,
        his five-fold lion-lineage,
he who has shed light on the darkness of grammar,
        he hath made my paths crooked.
I can be brave and I can be good
        Within my father's house, within my
funereal, phosphorescent light.

I dream that my father came back.
        Does the grave give up its dead?
kiss not the dead for they suffocate the living.
        (There thy father stands a'digging)

"And is that all?" I asked.
        The scent of lilac-bushes; on the bank?
Birds. Green forest. Space. And heat.
        For this the ancient stars were hurled,
as owls their moaning make?

3.

This is the dead fiddle. Look where the wood
                    fogs, clouds, mists, cones, peaks, precipices,
like the eyes of wolves
                    two thousand years ago.
And still our horses rustle like the rain.

4.

O who will kill the great Time-Moth?
                    Two thousand years, a little thing
This year am I five thousand years of age:
                    actions and thoughts and persons without number.

How good to stop.
                    A minute! Another minute!
I am released of grief's predicament
                    and walk around in unpatched shoes.
It is a known spot on an unknown star.
                    How are you, dear world, this morning?[8]

Epilogue: Mensch

My father ends his book with an epilogue beginning with the sentence "When I was a boy, all of my grandparents spoke Yiddish." He considers the Yiddish word *mensch*, (likely the only compliment he had heard in Yiddish) and remembers his grandparents squeezing his cheeks or hugging him, in a moment when he'd acted well, exclaiming, "Oy Mark, such a mensch you are!" This meant he was "a good boy" and "so grown up." He wants that from someone again, in the moment of his writing, from a person "with great integrity," he hopes, so the compliment would be meaningful. He imagines his readers as mensches: writing that "a mensch honors sorrow and loss as part of what naturally comes to all people and meets it where it is."

I shouldn't be surprised he ends the book this way, but I am. Ever the spiritual seeker, he had become a kind of Episcopalian when Joshua was alive, following an Episcopalian guru figure called "Murray," surely another Jew. My grandfather used to refer to him, scathingly, as "my son the Episcopalian." During my childhood, he settled on Sufism, meditated, even took a Sufi name, but when it came time for his death, he asked his friends to build him a coffin out of raw pine and drill holes in it, and was buried in a traditional Jewish shroud, shards of broken crockery over his eyes. Though he never acknowledged these traditions as Jewish ones, his choices for after his death closely resembled those of our ancestors. He ends the book as he ended his life: Jewishly. A mensch in a shroud, a good boy.

I remember meeting one of his grandmothers as a small child. I sat, once, in her kitchen. It bustled, with cookware, *tchotchkes*, radio in a jumble on top of the refrigerator. In my memory it glows orange with warmth. The whole place like a big earthy hug radiating love, so different from the assimilated German Jews on my mother's side of the family, who were tall and lean, with little softness to them. Even their kitchens were athletic; spare and tidy. My *Bubbe*'s white hair in a cloud of steam as she made me, for the first and only time in my life, *matzoh brei* fried in schmaltz. I can imagine how good it would have felt if she called me a mensch. The kitchen is the only room I remember—as if there were no other rooms, that one so full the rest of the house could have fallen into the sea.

I've been struggling to find a final excerpt from my father's book to include, but nothing seems good enough. Nothing is good enough. This may be in part because he didn't finish, and before I'm overly harsh about his skill with language (I have grown, among other things, kinder than I was at twenty-five) I remind myself that he worked on the book for less than a year, from Joshua's birthday in July 2005, through sickness, until his death just after my birthday in March 2006. Reading as a writer, I see how his desire to help and inspire readers who are grieving causes him to leap hurriedly into a teaching story, often right when he seemed at the precipice of describing his own experience in fresh, probably painful ways. Walter Benjamin would call this "memoire voluntaire," a kind of memory that has become an object, poetically sterile. Benjamin knew we don't lose the dead all at once. Or maybe I'm still not a good reader for his book, again reading as a child who only wants to know and be known by his father.

I flip through and keep seeing things I never saw, or couldn't take in. I never noticed that on page 170 he begins a chapter with an epigraph from a poem I wrote just after college. The lines, I swear, not shameful, but not worthy of reproducing here. But they must have meant something to him. The chapter is about going to Strawberry Mansion, the neighborhood in North Philadelphia where his grandparents lived during his childhood. In this chapter he describes driving around with his mother in 1993, trying to see where they'd lived, his grandparents' drugstore, only to find the neighborhood decayed and impoverished beyond recognition. In my opening essay I noted how little there was of his living children in the book, yet here he is quoting me, putting me beside his literary heroes, Mary Oliver, Euripides, Rumi, Hafiz.

I felt such erasure from his narrative—the longest mention of me is when I was one week old and had to return to the hospital with a bout of jaundice. He describes how traumatizing this was for him, and how he pulled away from feeling close to me after. And yet, he's quoting me— not the baby with whom I no longer share a name with, but me, Miller. He takes my lines back to 1993, before they were written. He moves me through time, just as I do with him now. Today I'd like to call him and read him Paul Celan—maybe "Line the Wordcaves."

Not only because it's one of my favorite poems, and it seems like, despite his love of poetry, my father never found his way to Celan's work, but because I think the way Celan describes the possibilities of language, of words themselves, speaks to something about there being space (and therefore time) in places we might not always look. For Celan, words can be caves, places to inhabit, "line" with "panther skins," explore. These caves (which are maybe our mouths?) can grow and change, be given gifts. I love the list of things the "wordcaves" are given, which speak to movement of different kinds. Exterior "courtyards" and interior "panther skins" and then "chambers," shocking extra space in the "drop doors." Finally, they are given "wildnesses": radical spaces of potential. "Wildnesses" are so much more than mere grounds or land. They are multiple, a-grammatically moving and building. Not "wilderness," which is, perhaps, just uninhabited space, but "wildnesses," which lack restraint and seem purposeful, unbounded, rebellious, full of wonder and possibility, and not just out there, but in here, not one, but many and uncountable.

I wanted to call you, and now I'm not sure how to stop calling. Celan was listening, and I am too. I'm listening, Papa, for our "second / and each time second and second / tone." I return to this poem often, and now I bring you with me. Wondering. Why is it always "second?" Three times, "second," as if sequence and linearity are broken, bent, or rejected. Whatever is next is just next, not one thing in a list of many, no matter how many there are. Two points, b ut never in a line. Two and always more, "each time," than two. The tone a kind of echo happening in "wordcaves" in time, and I'm missing you, each time.

Memoir Cento

They untape my eyes

I find myself not drowned

but endlessly drowning

My open right hand moves

through the flames, the quivering

of his little arms and legs

The garden breathes shallowly

We are unable to relax

around the baby, the liquid gurgling

sound of the red-winged blackbird high up

in the maple tree going konk la ree, konk la ree

Talk to me, Joshua.

It feels so lonely, this touching.

This most tender of pleasures

I walked all my children through croup,

bad dreams, and we'd wildly kiss and fall

on the ground and roll around together

ecstatically. Joshua, how could you leave me

bonded to a helpless thing, irretrievably lost.

Sailors describe a sailboat in still, windless

waters as being "in irons."

I carry many hurts at the hands of my father.

Jay grows more transparent every day,

I can almost see the sun shining right through him.

And the hands. Well, you've got to know

that even when nearing death,

Jewish people talk with their hands!

Streams of people, rivers

of people I've done wrongs to,

knowingly and unknowingly.

The Talmud teaches

when the Temple was destroyed

all the gates of heaven were closed

except one: the gate of tears.

I became history and I became water.

Dear Joshua, Happy thirty-first birthday

Sometimes it would be afternoon

before I realized. Dear Poppa

You can find me,

I am closer to you than blood.

In Joshua's arms, I am home,

he is in me now and forever

Joshua, today, dear boy.

Memoir Cento i

They untape   my eyes

      I find myself but endlessly

my hand through   the quivering

      his little arms and legs

shallowly   we are unable
        Joshua

the red-winged blackbird   konk la ree, konk la ree

          Joshua

this touching   this most tender   ecstatically

        Joshua
a thing   irretrievably

      a sailboat

"in irons"   the hands of my father

      transparent

and the hands   their hands!

      knowingly

and unknowingly   all the gates
        of heaven

history   and water
      dear Joshua

sometimes   it would be afternoon

dear Poppa

I am closer to you   than home

Joshua, today, dear boy

Memoir Cento ii

untape   my eyes

                  endlessly

my hand

                  we are unable
Joshua

        blackbird

                        Joshua

                  most tender

        Joshua

                        irretrievably

        a sail

                  the hands

        transparent

the hands   hands

                  all the gates

                  and water

dear Joshua

dear Poppa

Joshua,   dear

The Cake

The last time I saw my father
when we both were breathing

it was almost my birthday, the air
alive with lilacs, forsythias

rioting in the lane. A little wind
lifts the lace curtains my mother

hangs, invariably, in every window.
He doesn't like my birthday cake,

which is chocolate, and asks for *cake
like that*, pointing to a painting his friend

made: gold-white sphere surrounded
by deepest blue, which before then we

called his "go into the light" painting
and now call "the cake" painting.

I think he's looking at me but he's
looking past, to the window, where

they gather, do you see them? "No,"
I say, "tell me." *You don't see them? My*

father, the others? I saw only him
seeing them. The cake still tasted

good to me. I thought I knew
the difference between things

you could and couldn't touch.
A window frame, a wooden chair,

his soft sleeping shirt, the air.
"Papa," I say. *Papa*, he says.

NOTES ON THE ORIGIN AND SOURCES OF THE POEMS

1   All memoir sections originate from Mark Oberman's unpublished memoir, *Climbing the Joshua Tree: Awakening the Heart to Move through Sorrow*, a project interrupted by his death in March, 2006. In my father's book, he refers to his neighbors in Phoenixville as "Ed and Martha," while the *Pottstown Mercury*, the local paper, identifies the neighbor as "Arthur Nicol." I have been unable to account for this difference, and have left the discrepancy intact.

2   "Joshua's Birthday" borrows from Marcia Falk's "Blessing for Children," 124. Marcia Falk, *The Book of Blessings: New Jewish Prayers for Daily Life, the Sabbath, and the New Moon Festival*. Harper Collins: San Francisco, 1996.

3   "*Pottstown Mercury*, 1972" includes Joshua's obituary, originally found in the newspaper of the same name. "2-Year-Old Boy Drowns after Falling in Pool," *Pottstown Mercury*, September 19, 1972.

4   "Phoenixville, 2020" features a conversation between Dante and Ovid, with lines from *Inferno* and *Metamorphoses*. Dante, *Inferno*, trans. Mandelbaum; and Ovid, *Metamorphoses*, trans. Dryden.

Dante Alighieri, *The Divine Comedy*. Translated by Allen Mandelbaum. Everyman's Library/Alfred A. Knopf, New York, 1995. This poem borrows language from *Inferno*, Canto XXIV, 160–63.

Ovid, *Metamorphoses in 15 books, translated by Mr. Dryden, Mr. Addison, Dr. Garth, Mr. Mainwaring, Mr. Congreve, Mr. Rowe, Mr. Pope, Mr. Gay, Mr. Eusden, Mr. Croxall, and other eminent hands. Published by Sir Samuel Garth, M.D. Adorn'd with sculptures.* (London: Printed for J. and R. Tonson and S. Draper in the Strand, 1751; Ann Arbor, MI: Text Creation Partnership, 2011), book 1, 1 (trans. Dryden), https:// quod.libumich.edu/cgi/t/text/text-idx?c=ecco;cc=ecco;rgn=div1;view =text;idno=004871123.0001.000;node=004871123.0001.000:6 and book 15, 528–29 https://quod.lib.umich.edu/cgi/t/text/text-idx?c=ecco

;cc=ecco;rgn=div2;view=text;idno=004871123.0001.000;node
=004871123.0001.000:6.15.

5   "The Centaur" also borrows from Dante's *Inferno*. Dante Alighieri,
The Divine Comedy. Translated by Allen Mandelbaum. Everyman's
Library/Alfred A. Knopf, New York, 1995.

6   The section "Field Cento" in the poem "The Field" is composed of
lines from Donald Hall, "Name the Horses," Angela Shaw, "Children in
a Field," Carol Moldaw, "The Lightning Field," Louise Glück, "Withch-
grass," Robert Duncan, "Often I Am Permitted to Return to a Meadow,"
Randall Mann, "?," Robert Frost, "The Mountain," Wallace Stevens,
"July Mountain," Terrance Hayes, "Upright Blues," Thomas Lux, "Chil-
dren in School During Heavy Snowfall," Ellen Bryant Voigt, "*Kyrie*,"
Gabriel Spera, "In a Field Outside the Town," Leila Wilson, "What Is
the Field," Will Alexander, "Towards the Primeval Lightning Field,"
Walt Whitman, "Vigil Strange I Kept on the Field One Night," Elise Pas-
chen, "I Will Leave You in Possession of the Field," Wallace Stevens,
"Frogs Eat Butterflies. Snakes Eat Frogs. Hogs Eat Snakes. Men Eat
Hogs.," Wyatt Townley, "The Breathing Field," Laura Newbern, "The
Sea," Larissa Szporluk, "Solar Wind," Robert Duncan, "The Opening of
the Field," Florence Randal Livesay, "Old Folk Songs of Ukraina," Rumi
(translated by Coleman Barks), "Out Beyond Ideas of Wrongdoing and
Rightdoing," George Szirtes, "My Father Carries Me Across a Field,"
and Natalie Diaz, "From the Desire Field."

7   "Two Shabbats with Paul Celan" and "Epilogue: Mensch" borrow
from Pierre Joris's translations of Paul Celan. *Celan, Breathturn into
Timestead; The Collected Later Poetry: A Bilingual Edition*. Translated
by Pierre Joris. Farrar, Straus and Giroux: New York, 2014.

8   "Jewish Cento, 1957" is composed entirely from lines from Nathan
and Marynn Ausubel's anthology *A Treasury of Jewish Poetry from Bib-
lical Times to Present*. New York: Crown Publishers Inc., 1957. Lines
are from the following poets, quoted in order of how they appear in the
cento: Nahman of Bratzlav, "The Heart of the World," Stanley Kunitz,
"Reflection by a Mailbox," Karl Wolfskehl, "We Go," Muriel Rukeyser,
"Madboy's Song," Louis Ginsberg, "Soon at Last My Sighs and Moans,"

Stanley Burnshaw, "Bread," César Tiempo (translated from the Spanish by Donald Devenish Walsh), "Harangue on the Death of Hayyim Nahman Bialik," Jules Alan Wein, "Genesis," Abraham M. Klein, "Haggadah," Joseph Ezobi, "A Barren Soul," Rachel (translated from the Hebrew by L. V. Snowman), "Barren," Karl Wolfskehl, "To Be Said at the Seder," Zalman Schneour (translated from the Yiddish by Joseph Leftwich), "Cherries," The Second Isaiah, "Comfort Ye, Comfort Ye My People," Maxwell Bodenheim, "Poem," Muriel Rukeyser, "Even During War," Norman Rosten, "Out of Our Shame," line from Avinu Malkeinu (by an unknown medieval poet), "Lines from Avinu Malkeinu," Eleazar ben Kalir, "The Terrible Sons," Abraham Sutzkever (translated from the Yiddish by Joseph Leftwich), "Here I Am," César Tiempo (translated from the Spanish by Donald Devenish Walsh), "I Tell of Another Young Death," Karl Shapiro, "V Letter," Leib Olitski (translated from the Yiddish by Jacob Sonntag), "My Song to the Jewish People," Rachel Morpurgo (translated from the Hebrew by Nina Davis Salaman), "Song," Jon Silkin, "A Space in the Air," Emma Lazarus, "The Banner of the Jew," unknown poet (from the Epitaph for Elijah Levita), "Epitaph for Elijah Levita," Jeremiah Ben Hilkiah, (from the Book of Lamentations 3:1–15), "From the Book of Lamentations," Zalman Schneour (translated from the Yiddish by Joseph Leftwich), "Besieged," Carl Zuckmayer (translated from the German by E. B. Ashton), "My Death," Isidor Schneider, "Insects," unknown poet (translated from the Yiddish by Joseph Leftwich), "I Sit with my Dolls," Mani Leib (translated from the Yiddish by Joseph Leftwich), "Door and Window Bolted Fast," Marcel Schwob (translated from the French by William Brown Meloney), "Things Dead," David Nomberg (translated from the Yiddish by Alter Brody), "A Russian Cradle Song," James Oppenheim, "The Future," Hugo Von Hofmannsthal (translated from the German by Charles Wharton Stork), "A Vision," Alexander Bezymensky (translated from the Russian by Babette Deutsch), "Village and Factory," Israel Zangwil, "Evolution," Meir of Rothenburg, Germany, 1215–1293 (translated from the Hebrew by Nina Davis Salaman), "The Burning of the Law," Humbert Wolfe, "The Dead Fiddle," André Spire (translated from the French by Jethro Bithell), "Lonely," Nachum Yud (translated from the Yiddish by Joseph Leftwich), "Like the Eyes of Wolves," Alter Brody, "Lamentations," Rainer Maria Rilke, "The Youth Dreams," Benjamin De Casseres, "Moth-Terror," Judah Leib Gordon (translated from the Hebrew by Alice Lucas and Helena Frank), "Simhat Torah," Delmore Schwartz, "Look, in the Labyrinth of Memory," Antoni Slonimski (translated from the Polish by Watson Kirkconnell), "Morning and Evening," Charles Reznikoff, "The Lamps Are Burning," Ilya Ehrenburg (translated from the Russian by Babette Deutsch), "The Sons of Our Sons," Martin Feinstein, "Burning Bush," Franz Werfel (translated from the German by Jacob Sloan), "Teach Us to Mark This, God," Babette Deutsch, "Scene with Figure," Horace Traubel, "How Are You, Dear World, This Morning."

ACKNOWLEDGMENTS

I am grateful to the following for publishing poems from this project (sometimes in an earlier form) and grateful to their editors and readers: The *Academy of American Poets Poem-a-Day series*, *EOAGH*, *Foglifter*, *Hopkins Review*, *Jewish Currents*, *NECK*, *New Yorker*, and *Poetry*.

Thank you to the New York Foundation for the Arts for the 2023 New York Foundation for the Arts/New York State Council on the Arts Fellowship for supporting this work.

Unending gratitude to those who have encouraged, uplifted, and lovingly edited me during this project, in writing and in life: Seth and Aisha Anderson-Oberman, Ellen Bass, Elizabeth Bradfield, Judith Butler, Marcy Coburn, Owen Colás, Bran Fenner, Elizabeth Freeman, Alice Friman, Sheyam Ghieth, Abe Greenhouse, Jack Halberstam, Maria Dahvana Headley, Marwa Helal, Margie Housley, Marie Howe, Rosemary Irving, Trudie Kaiser, Anjali Khosla, Scott Korb, Rickey Laurentiis, Nathan Levitt, Amara Lillien-Sterling, Ricardo Maldonado, Dora Malech, Laura Newbern, Elijah Oberman, Susan Oberman, Penelope Pelizzon, Jules Aviv Rose, Michael and Andy Rosen-Pyros, Helen Betya Rubinstein, Bureen Ruffin, Claire Schwartz, Leah Schwebel, Shawn Setaro, Claire Solomon, Louisa Solomon, Mark Solomon, Nicole Solomon, Julia Tillinghast, Rae Angelo Tutera, Wendy Xu, and May Ye. I'm grateful to my colleagues and students at Lang College, who give me ridiculous hope for the future, and to Mildred and Moishe Solomon ל״ז and 4 Lake Drive, where much of this book was written and revised.

Enormous thanks Ryan Kendall, Dave Rainey, Bird Williams, Ken Wissoker, and the team at Duke University Press for all your hard work on behalf of this book, and for believing in me and in this project. It truly means more to me than I can say.